The Power of Belief in Business

W. Ryan Harmon

Author's Note

My name is William Ryan Harmon, and I was born
and raised in Huntington, WV where I came from
humble beginnings. My father worked day and
night as a maintenance mechanic to provide a
stable life for my two brothers, mother, and
I. My parents were two of my best friends
growing up, and they taught me that with enough
belief, a person can achieve anything. My mother
and father constantly painted a vision that
someday I would get a college education, become a
successful professional, and provide a stable
life for my wife and children. Years later, the
vision that they painted came true. I am a
loving husband, the father of five beautiful
children, and I have received six promotions
in my nine year career with a Fortune 1000
Company. I owe my personal and professional
success to what I refer to as "The Power of
Belief", but what started as a mother and father
simply encouraging their child to relentlessly go
after his dreams.

Table of Contents

Section 1:
Introduction

Why did I write this book?

I have spent my career trying to understand what makes the difference between successful and unsuccessful managers. I consider myself lucky that I was given the opportunity to work with and for both types of managers along the way. Yes, you read that correctly. When you are working to develop your own management style, it is great to study what works and does not work for others. At times, it was painful, but I did not let any of these learning opportunities pass me by.

There were also times that it was extremely confusing. The strategies that provided positive results for the successful manager would be attempted by the unsuccessful manager with poor results. How could the same strategy have such different outcomes? It appeared that the results had more to do with the manager than with the strategy itself. Could this explain why some of my own strategies were unsuccessful? I decided to dig deeper into the changes that I could make as a manager, and to my surprise, as I changed, the team's results significantly improved.

I knew that I was on to something, but at the time, I was not aware of how big it actually was. The more that I discovered; the more questions that I began to ask myself. Why fire when you can inspire? Is it possible that managers do not truly understand the causes for mediocre performance? Do we pass blame on to employees when we should accept responsibility ourselves? Are we doing our companies and our employees a great injustice? As I continued to learn and develop my understanding of what makes a successful manager, I came to the following realization.

You can **force** your employees to **perform the minimum requirements** or you can **allow** them to **achieve unprecedented success**. When employees are afraid of losing their jobs, they will only do enough to keep themselves out of trouble.

Why would employees take risks and have an innovative mindset if they feel that making a mistake could be detrimental to their career or could result in retaliation or embarrassment? **THEY WON'T!**

When your customers work directly with your discouraged employees, will they have a positive impression of your company? **THEY WON'T!**

Will discouraged employees come up with innovative product and service solutions to improve the customer's experience? **THEY WON'T!**

Will your company be able to have sustainable, long-term, profitable growth? **IT CAN'T!**

If your goal is to have a successful business with motivated employees that take excellent care of your customers to ensure sustainable, long-term, profitable growth, you are reading the right book! This book will walk you through the critical steps required to improve the way that you manage your business.

Albert Einstein referred to insanity as doing things the same way multiple times and expecting different results. If your business is not achieving the results that you desire, changes must occur before you can expect to see improvements. Are you willing to change in order to permit maximum results?

Section 2: A New Mindset

The Theory of Belief

Maslow's Hierarchy of Needs is a theory written by Abraham Maslow, and it states that human beings are motivated by unsatisfied needs. He states that lower level needs need to be satisfied before you can satisfy higher level needs. On the surface, this seems to be accurate, but with careful evaluation, it is evident that something is missing.

I agree completely with the order in which Abraham Maslow presented his theory. Under normal circumstances, an individual would rely on these basic levels (physiological, safety, love, esteem, self-actualization) to guide their decision-making, but there must be something that keeps these levels in balance. Below, I have illustrated the power of belief.

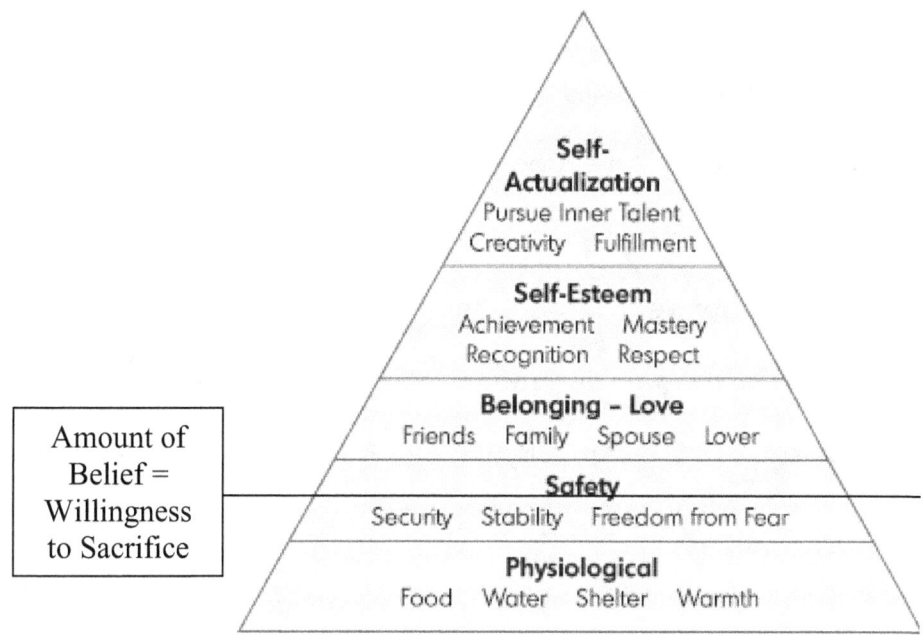

After reviewing the illustration above, the logic should start to become more obvious. My "Theory of Belief" states that people will sacrifice their needs up to the point that their sacrifice exceeds their level of belief. In the absence of belief, people will base make decisions based on Maslow's Hierarchy of Needs, but if enough belief is present, people will sacrifice those needs.

Belief has a large influence on the way we respond to life's many challenging obstacles and on the decisions that we make each day. As our levels of belief increase, we will sacrifice more to achieve the desired results even though it is against our human nature. This is an area of great concern, because the exact opposite effect occurs as we decrease our levels of belief. For example, if an employee has a strong commitment to and belief in their leader, they may achieve great results, but if you replace that leader with an individual that they despise; there is a good chance that the results will reflect this change in leadership.

The paths that people follow and the decisions that they make are guided by their belief in something or someone, but what if their belief was taken away? What if you could disprove all of their beliefs? Would they change the way that they live and respond to life's many challenges? I believe that they would. The following pages contain a brief description of each level of Maslow's Hierarchy of Needs, but I will go one step further to show how belief, when present, over-rides our human nature.

PHYSIOLOGICAL NEEDS

Physiological needs are our most basic needs; such as air, food, sleep, water, and sex. When we do not satisfy these needs, we are motivated to alleviate these needs as quickly as possible. Maslow believed that we will not think of other needs until these needs are fulfilled, and with this, I partially agree. Under normal circumstances, we would definitely require that these needs were being met before thinking of anything else, but what if it jeopardized our belief?

Theory of Belief Example

Have you ever heard of a soldier that was taken prisoner by the enemy? Do most people forfeit valuable information to keep from being deprived of their physiological needs? The majority of people would forfeit this information if they did not have a strong belief in what they were doing. What if a soldier felt that by sacrificing his life and well-being, he could save the rest of his/her unit and help accomplish the mission? If we were to follow the Hierarchy of Needs, it would imply that regardless of his belief in the mission, concern for his/her troops, or desire to protect his/her homeland, this soldier would only think of satisfying his/her physiological needs. If this is true, how can we account for an act of bravery? How do we explain a person giving their own life for the good of the mission and protection of his/her unit?

SAFETY NEEDS

If the physiological needs are relatively well met, there then arises a new set of needs, which we may describe as the safety needs. These needs could be described as security, stability, and freedom from fear. Surely no one would sacrifice these needs due to belief, would they?

Theory of Belief Example

Have you ever heard of a suicide attack? Many of these attacks involve an individual that sacrifices their own life due to a strong belief in something (i.e. religion, political, etc). By examining these extreme actions, it is easier to understand how much of an influence that belief has on all of us. We may not take it to this extreme, but belief plays a significant role in each of our lives.

BELONGING AND LOVE

When physiological needs and safety needs are met, we begin to think about belonging and love needs. You begin to feel the need for family, friends, and/or a lover. Obviously, a

person would not sacrifice these needs, would
they?

Theory of Belief Example

Have you ever known someone that stayed
in an abusive relationship, because they
believed that they could "change" the other
person? What about a person who sacrifices
their relationships with their family and
friends in order to stay with the abuser?
People will sacrifice almost anything,
including their love and belonging needs, if
they have a strong enough belief. If belief
were taken out of the equation, people would
immediately leave abusive relationships, but
unfortunately, it is easier for someone on
the outside to see what is happening than
the person who is involved in the unhealthy
relationship.

SELF-ESTEEM NEEDS

When physiological, safety, and love and belonging needs are met, we move on to self-esteem needs. These are the need for achievement, recognition, mastery, and fulfillment. Have you seen an example of someone who sacrificed their self-esteem needs for a great cause?

Theory of Belief Example

In April of 2006, I was promoted to the position of Branch Manager in Paducah, Kentucky. I was tasked with the challenging job of starting a new location and virtually building it from the ground up. I voluntarily worked seven days a week for several months to get the location off of the ground. I was exhausted and physically sick on many occasions, but my belief in my company kept me moving forward. The strangest thing about this situation is that it was contagious. People would offer to help with areas outside of their responsibilities, they would work long hours, and it was all because of their belief in what we were working to accomplish. During this process, I was ridiculed, blamed for setbacks, and my confidence was challenged, but I was able to hold onto my belief and to keep pushing forward. Have you ever sacrificed yourself for something that you believe in? If the answer is yes, you have experienced the power of belief.

SELF-ACTUALIZATION

These needs involve the desire to fulfill your potential and become important after successfully fulfilling the four lower level needs. According to Maslow, only a small percentage of people are actually self-actualizing.

<u>Theory of Belief Example</u>

This is an area of great importance, because by properly utilizing the Theory of Belief, you can move yourself towards self-actualization. How can you get somewhere if you do not know where you want to go? You have to have a plan or a road map or you may not like where you end up. According to the "Theory of Belief", you should create a vision of where you want to be in the future and the steps that you are going to take to get there. By having an action plan, you can better understand how challenging events are worth finishing. You can fight through setbacks, over-come obstacles, and succeed against the most difficult challenges if you continuously refill your "Belief Tank".

Taking the "Right" Point of View

"IF YOU WANT PEOPLE TO ACHIEVE MAXIMUM RESULTS, YOU MUST STRIVE TO PROVIDE THEM WITH ALL OF THEIR NEEDS, BUT IF YOU WANT A PERSON TO PERFORM EVEN WHEN DEPRIVED OF THOSE NEEDS, THEY MUST HAVE A STRONG BELIEF IN THE CAUSE."

As a manager, you have two options when it comes to overcoming challenges and achieving maximum results. First, you can "attempt" to remove all of the challenges and obstacles that stand in the way of your employees. I say attempt, because this option would be great if it were possible. No matter how hard you work, you cannot make your employees' lives perfect. Second, you can work to build a strong enough belief in the cause that the employees will sacrifice anything to achieve it. This also sounds like a winner, but it is not realistic. The only logical approach is a combination of the two, and it can only be achieved if you take the "Right" point of view.

You must look upon any goal, obstacle, or challenge with the appropriate perspective. This can be difficult, because your employee's obstacles and challenges may sound more like excuses than valid concerns and your customer's complaints may seem trivial. You must force yourself to look at it through their eyes. It does not matter if you think the concern is valid or not, because it is valid to them, and their perception is their reality.

Below is an illustration of how some managers view their employees' obstacles and challenges.

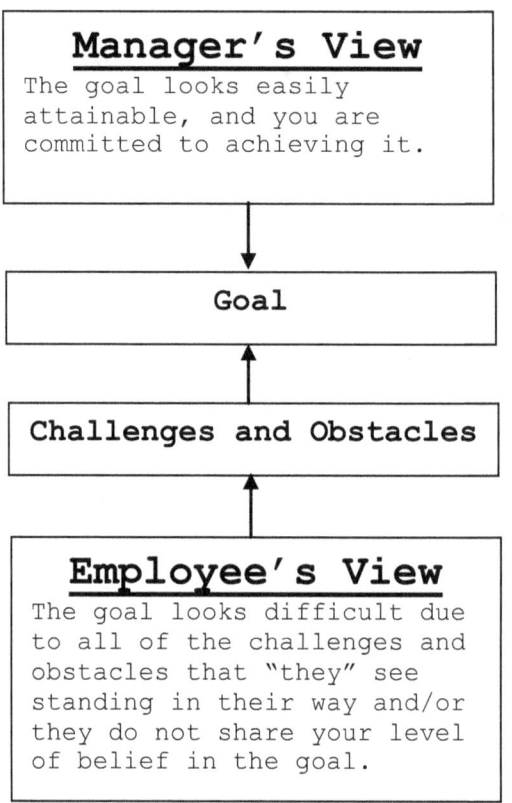

The following steps will help you take the

"Right" point of view. Step 1, consult the

employee to get their point of view, because many

of the obstacles and challenges may not be

visible to you. Step 2, remove as many of the

challenges and obstacles as possible to help the

employee achieve the goal. Step 3, continuously

communicate the vision to increase the employee's

belief in the goal. This will help give the

partner the strength to work through the

remaining challenges.

Below is an illustration of how some companies

view their customers' concerns and complaints.

Company's View

The customer's concerns seem trivial and their complaints are unfounded. The company is focused on removing their own challenges and obstacles.

↓

Company's Challenges and Obstacles

↓

Company's Goals

Customer's Goal

↑

Customer's Challenges and Obstacles

↑

Customer's View

The goal looks difficult due to all of the challenges and obstacles that "they" see standing in their way and they do not have a full understanding of how to achieve the results.

The following steps will help you take the "Right" point of view. Step 1, consult the customer to get their point of view, because many of the obstacles and challenges may not be visible to you. Step 2, make recommendations for improvements and assist the customer in determining the right products/services for their business needs. Step 3, work with the customer to improve their understanding of how to use the product/service effectively.

As you can see from the illustrations above, it is extremely important to look at any goal from the right perspective. The best person to give you insight on the challenges of accomplishing a goal is likely to be the person that performs the task on a daily basis or the customer that uses your products/services to achieve their own business objectives. You have a vested interest in helping your employees and customers achieve their goals. Successful employees make your organization more effective and successful customers keep your organization

in business.

Five Points of Business Belief

After reviewing the previous sections, you have obtained a basic understanding of the theory of belief and the importance of taking the right point of view. Next, we will review the power of belief in business and how you can use the theory of belief to determine the areas that require improvement in your organization.

Belief in business is divided into five points; belief in the leader, belief in self, belief in the cause, belief in the team, and belief of the customer. I have included an illustration of this on the following page.

100% BELIEF= 100% BELIEF IN EACH OF THE 5 POINTS

To achieve maximum results, it is your responsibility to increase the levels of belief in each of the five points. To increase belief in any area, you must understand the level of belief that exists today; therefore, it is invaluable to have a quantifiable evaluation system for each of the five points. A sample evaluation system is listed below.

EACH QUESTION = 20 POINTS OUT OF 100 POINTS

POSSIBLE (INCREASE IN INCREMENTS OF 5 FOR

EACH SCORE)-EXAMPLE: IF YOU SCORE ADEQUATE STAFFING AS A 3, THIS WOULD EQUAL 3 X 5 PTS = 15 PTS TOWARDS THE TOTAL SCORE FOR BELIEF IN THE LEADER. IF YOU SCORE AQEQUATE STAFFING AS A 0, THIS WOULD EQUAL 0 X 5 PTS = 0 PTS TOWARDS THE TOTAL SCORE FOR BELIEF IN THE LEADER.

1. Method to evaluate the level of belief in the leader. (0-strongly disagree, 1-disagree, 2-somewhat agree, 3-agree, 4-strongly agree)

   a. The team is adequately staffed. (0, 1, 2, 3, 4)

      i. See Section 3: Get Staffed and Stay Staffed

   b. Your manager truly cares about you. (0, 1, 2, 3, 4)

      i. See Section 3: Care About your People

   c. Your manager treats you with honesty and respect. (0, 1, 2, 3, 4)

i. See Section 3: Honesty is
Essential

d. You are encouraged to take calculated
risks to improve overall performance.
(0, 1, 2, 3, 4)

i. See Section 3: Eliminate
Intimidation and Encourage
Innovation

e. You receive adequate training and
mentoring to develop you for future
opportunities. (0, 1, 2, 3, 4)

i. See Section 3: Don't Hold Them
Back

2. Method to evaluate the level of belief in
the cause? (0-strongly disagree, 1-
disagree, 2-somewhat agree, 3-agree, 4-
strongly agree)

a. Achieving the goals of the team
assists me in achieving my own
personal goals. (0, 1, 2, 3, 4)

  i. See Section 4: Start with their

   Goals

b. I am aware of the vision and fully

 understand it. (0, 1, 2, 3, 4)

  i. See Section 4: The Vision Must

   be Clear

c. Top goals are broken down into

 smaller goals that are fully

 understood and a game plan is in

 place to improve each of these lower

 level goals. (0, 1, 2, 3, 4)

  i. See Section 4: Incremental Goals

   Identified

d. The established goals are attainable.

 (0, 1, 2, 3, 4)

  i. See Section 4: The Vision Must

   be Attainable

e. The best idea wins instead of the

 manager dictating the direction. (0,

 1, 2, 3, 4)

        i. See Section 4: Agreement Must
Occur

3. Method to evaluate the level of belief in self? (0-strongly disagree, 1-disagree, 2-somewhat agree, 3-agree, 4-strongly agree)

    a. I have the knowledge and skill to successfully perform my job. (0, 1, 2, 3, 4)

        i. See Section 5: Adequate Knowledge and Skills

    b. I am comfortable voicing my viewpoint to the team and to my manager. (0, 1, 2, 3, 4)

        i. See Section 5: Comfortable Voicing Viewpoint

    c. I have the appropriate tools to perform my job, and I fully understand how to use these tools successfully. (0, 1, 2, 3, 4)

        i. See Section 5: Tools for the Job

d. I have a system to stay organized and ensure that I do not miss deadlines. (0, 1, 2, 3, 4)

    i. See Section 5: System of Organization

e. I have the confidence in myself to take educated risks to improve overall performance. (0, 1, 2, 3, 4)

    i. See Section 5: Improvement Mindset

4. Method to evaluate the level of belief in the team. (0-strongly disagree, 1-disagree, 2-somewhat agree, 3-agree, 4-strongly agree)

a. Team members are in positions that are suitable for their knowledge and skills. (0, 1, 2, 3, 4)

    i. See Section 6: Right Players, Right Positions?

b. Team members are dedicated to achieving the goals. (0, 1, 2, 3, 4)

        i. See Section 6: Follow-Up System Required

c. Team members are consistently working to improve the performance of the team. (0, 1, 2, 3, 4)

        i. See Section 6: Improvement-Seeking Attitude Required

d. Team members are willing to share their strengths to improve the team's performance. (0, 1, 2, 3, 4)

        i. See Section 6: Encourage the Sharing of Strengths

e. Team members honestly and openly communicate on a regular basis. (0, 1, 2, 3, 4)

        i. See Section 6: "Scheduled" Open Communication

5. Method to evaluate the level of belief of the customer. (0-strongly disagree, 1-disagree, 2-somewhat agree, 3-agree, 4-strongly agree)

a. The vendor provides a quality product/service that is needed by our company. (0, 1, 2, 3, 4)

   i. See Section 7: Product

b. The vendor's products/services are provided at a fair cost to our company. (0, 1, 2, 3, 4)

   i. See Section 7: Value

c. The vendor takes the time to make sure that we understand how to use their products/services effectively, and they proactively offer other products, services, and ideas to improve our company. (0, 1, 2, 3, 4)

   i. See Section 7: Simplification

d. The vendor provides excellent service to our company. (0, 1, 2, 3, 4)

   i. See Section 7: Service

e. I trust that the vendor is honest and ethical in their business practices. (0, 1, 2, 3, 4)

i. See Section 7: Trust

First, we will review business belief without considering the belief of the customer. Distribute sections 1 through 4 to each of your employees, and ask them to honestly answer each question. Explain that the individual results will remain confidential and this tool will only be used to determine improvement initiatives in the future. If your employees are not comfortable with this exercise, you should allow them to anonymously answer the questions. After you receive the completed surveys, you should calculate each individual's results and an average score for the team. I have provided an example of this on the next page.

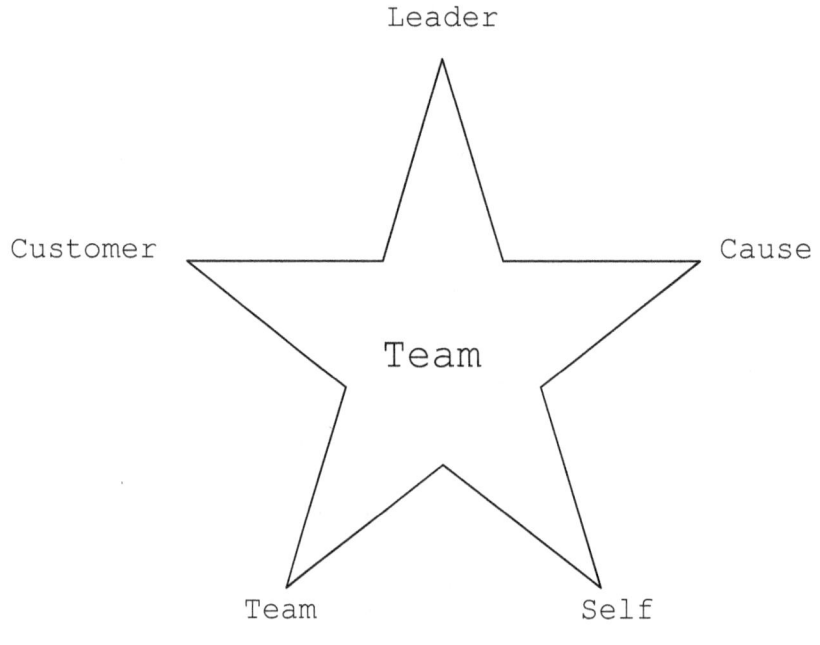

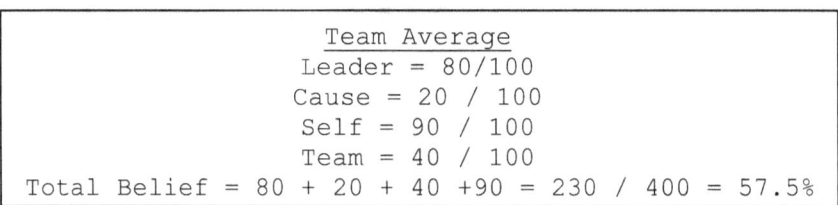

Team Average
Leader = 80/100
Cause = 20 / 100
Self = 90 / 100
Team = 40 / 100
Total Belief = 80 + 20 + 40 +90 = 230 / 400 = 57.5%

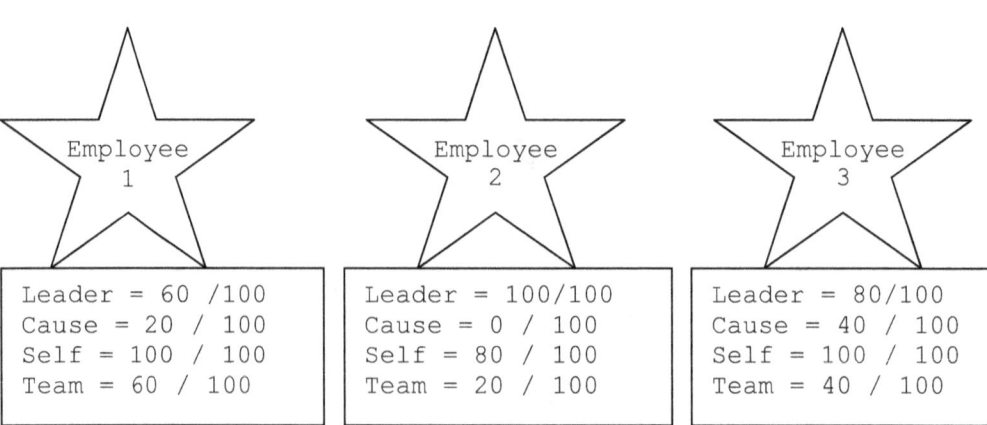

Employee 1	Employee 2	Employee 3
Leader = 60 /100	Leader = 100/100	Leader = 80/100
Cause = 20 / 100	Cause = 0 / 100	Cause = 40 / 100
Self = 100 / 100	Self = 80 / 100	Self = 100 / 100
Team = 60 / 100	Team = 20 / 100	Team = 40 / 100

As you can see from the illustration above, this team has a strong belief in their leader and in their own personal abilities, but they do not share the same level of belief in their team members or the cause that they are trying to achieve. This tool can help you determine which areas require your immediate attention. In the example above, you should invest more time on team building exercises and to increase belief in the cause than you should spend on the other two points.

Now we will review the same business and take the customers' belief into consideration. You can determine your customers' belief by contacting them and having them grade your company on the areas identified in section 5 of the evaluation system. There may be several ways to obtain this information from your customers (i.e. phone calls, mail surveys, etc); therefore, you should use the method that works the best for your organization. After you receive the completed surveys, you should calculate each customer's results and an average score for all of the customers.   I have provided an example of this below.

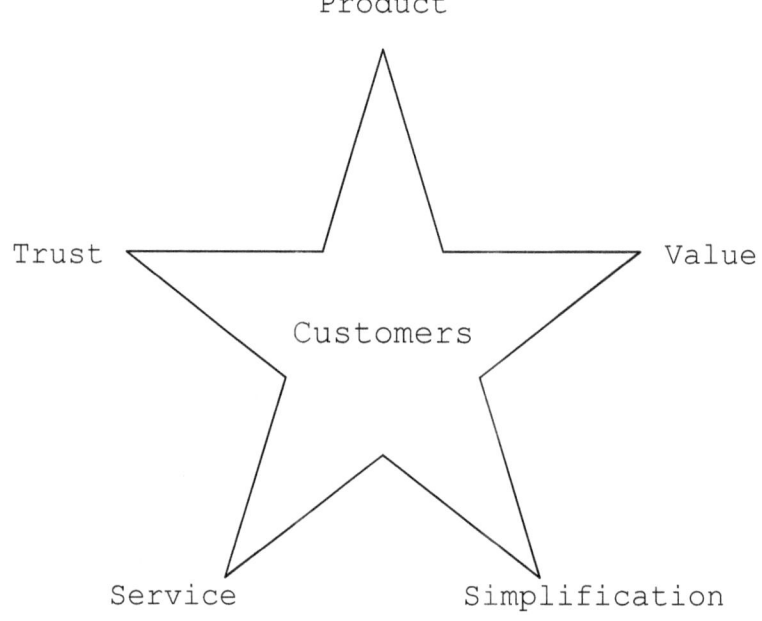

Product

Trust   Value

Customers

Service   Simplification

Customer Average
Product = 60/100
Value = 80/100
Simplification = 40/100
Service = 60/100
Trust = 80/100
Total Belief = 60 + 80 + 40 + 60 + 80 = 320 / 500 = 64%

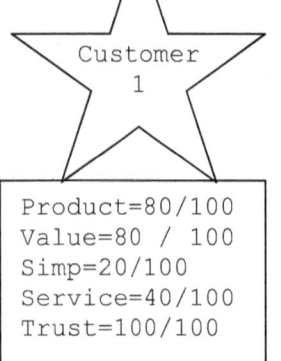

Customer 1

Product=80/100
Value=80 / 100
Simp=20/100
Service=40/100
Trust=100/100

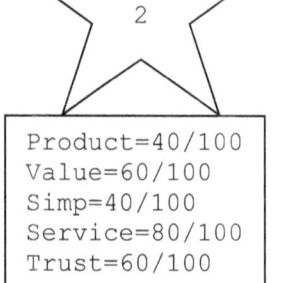

Customer 2

Product=40/100
Value=60/100
Simp=40/100
Service=80/100
Trust=60/100

Customer 3

Product=60/100
Value=100/100
Simp=60/100
Service=60/100
Trust=80/100

As you can see from the illustration on the previous page, these customers believe that they are receiving a valuable product/service, and they trust the company that provides it. The main focus points, in this example, should be given to simplification and to improving your products and services. You must evaluate and understand the belief levels of your customers, because without their belief, your business cannot succeed. The following example incorporates all five points of belief in business based on the examples above.

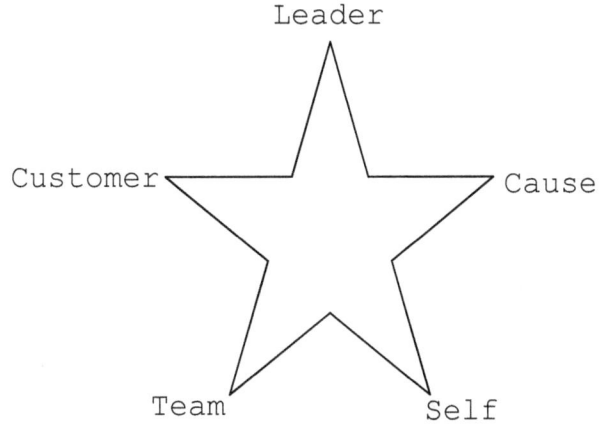

```
             Total Belief
          Leader = 80/100
          Cause = 20 / 100
          Team = 40 / 100
          Self = 90 / 100
        Customer = 64 / 100
80 + 20 + 40 + 90 + 64 = 294 / 500 = 58.8%
```

You cannot simply evaluate the levels of belief that your customers and employees have and expect your organization to improve. You can use the information that you obtain from your evaluations to implement improvement initiatives that take your company to the next level. The following sections are designed to give you a better understanding of how to improve each of the five points of belief.

Section 3: Belief in the Leader

Get Staffed
and Stay
Staffed

Don't
Hold
Them
Back

Leader

Care
About
Your
People

Eliminate
Intimidation and
Encourage
Innovation

Honesty is
Essential

The team is adequately staffed.
Get Staffed and Stay Staffed

Achieving and maintaining adequate staffing must be one of your top priorities or it will be difficult to have great success. How do you know if you are under-staffed, fully-staffed, or over-staffed? Do not be surprised if you cannot immediately answer that question. I spent a lot of time reviewing this question prior to coming to the following conclusion.

The staffing requirements for your business depend on the vision that you have for the future. For example, if your goal is to maintain your current customer base and improve the bottom line, you may need fewer employees than a business with growth as their primary objective. A business with growth as a priority would require additional sales representatives to increase their business as well as additional employees in training to fill positions added in the future.

ADEQUATE STAFFING

Regardless of your vision, you have to obtain and maintain adequate staffing for your business to be a long-term success. Your vision dictates what you can consider adequate staffing. It is extremely important to understand your staffing requirements, because when you are over-staffed, you cannot afford mistakes, but when you are under-staffed, you cannot avoid mistakes. You have to find a balance that will allow your team to consistently achieve the requirements set forth in your vision without breaking the bank. You owe it to your team to become and remain adequately staffed to allow them to perform the essential functions of their jobs successfully.

QUESTIONS TO EVALUATE STAFFING

The following five questions can help you determine if you have a solid system in place to maintain the appropriate staffing levels for your business.

1. Do you have a documented vision of what you want to achieve? (Profit, Growth, etc)

    a. It will be difficult to achieve your desired results if you have not identified where you want to go. By establishing a vision of where you want to go, you can determine who and what you need to get there.

2. Have you identified the type of person that you want to hire? (Personality type, Work Experience, Education, etc)

    a. If you do not know who you are looking for, it will not be easy to know when you have found the right person. Taking the time to document exactly what type of person you are looking for will increase your chances of recognizing that person when you find them. For example, I would prefer to have someone with less experience and a lot of enthusiasm than a person with a lot of experience and little enthusiasm. By knowing this in advance, I can quickly eliminate any candidate that does not exhibit an enthusiastic attitude.

3. Have you ranked your team members? (Top, Middle, Bottom, etc)

   a. This exercise can help you more efficiently run your business. First, identify your top performers and evaluate these employees to determine why they are successful. Next, you can identify your middle performers, and you can work with

them in their areas of weakness to
improve their performance. Finally,
you should identify the bottom
performers on your team to determine
the appropriate action steps to take.
If the employee is capable of doing
the work, and they refuse to
contribute, you need to replace that
employee. If the employee does not
have the skills to do the work, you
should work with them to develop
their skills or find another area
that best suits their skill set.

4. Do you have a documented system in place
to identify, recruit, and evaluate
candidates? (Interview guides, job
postings, testing, etc)

    a. Having a system in place to identify,
    recruit, and evaluate candidates is
    extremely beneficial. This can make
    the difficult task of recruiting and

hiring the best possible candidate much easier to accomplish. It can also save you time along the way if you know where to look, who you are looking for, and how you are going to determine which person is the most qualified for the position.

5. Do you have a system in place to develop your employees? (Training, Mentoring, etc).

   a. It is important to have a system in place to develop your employees. Having a documented training system and scheduled mentoring sessions will help develop your employees as well as your relationships with your employees. They will be less likely to become overwhelmed if they are properly prepared, and when they do "hit the wall", they will have you there to help them through the difficult times. Many times, it is better to keep and develop your current employees than it is to identify, recruit, hire, and train their replacements.

After reviewing the five questions above, you should have a better idea of the areas that you want to implement changes and improvements. Properly staffing your team gives everyone the opportunity to be successful, and it will prepare your business for future challenges and opportunities.

Your manager truly cares about you.
Care About your People

Caring about your people can have a dramatic effect on the morale, attendance, turnover, and overall success of your business. It is important to understand that this does not mean acting as if you care about them. You must have a genuine concern for their wellbeing, show it on a consistent basis, treat everyone with respect, believe your people, believe in your people, and have an unselfish attitude.

GENUINE CONCERN

You can show a genuine concern for your employee's wellbeing by taking the time to get to know them better. Finding out that they like to do for fun and what sports they enjoy may seem trivial and unrelated to your business objectives, but that is the furthest thing from the truth. By knowing what makes your employees "tick", together you can develop a game plan to help them achieve their own personal goals while improving the organization. Here are a few ways to show a genuine concern for your employees.

1. Remember their birthday and anniversary.

2. Perform Random Acts of Kindness (something nice for no reason)

3. Tell them that you appreciate them.

4. Do not take credit for something that they have done. Recognize them for their achievements, and give them the appropriate credit.

5. Know how they like to spend their leisure time and discuss it with them.

It is critical to understand that you can eliminate several positive interactions with one negative event. Therefore, it is imperative that you consistently show a genuine concern for your employees. It has been stated that people do not care how much you know until they know how much you care. This is very true, and to prove that you truly care, you must show genuine concern on a consistent basis. Have you ever fallen into the inconsistency traps listed below?

1.   You usually welcome your employees' questions, but you are having a very bad day. Your employee comes to you with a question, and you act as if their concern is not important by reacting in a rude manner. You may apologize to your employee in the future, but the next time your employee has a question, they may not come to you for the answer.

2.   You normally congratulate your employees on their birthdays and anniversaries. You were not feeling well today, and you did not take the time to write that note or personally tell the person congratulations. This may seem like a minor issue, but to that employee, they may feel that

they are not as appreciated as the other employees.

3.   You normally do not allow your employees to take an early lunch. An employee that you really like approaches you with the same request, and you allow him/her to leave thirty minutes early. Although your intentions may be completely harmless, this could be interpreted as favoritism and negatively impact your team's morale.

TREAT EVERYONE WITH RESPECT

Another component of caring about your people is treating everyone with respect. You must have the mentality that everyone is important to the overall success of the business, and you must emphasize this point with your actions. If you treat everyone with equal respect, it can become contagious and change the atmosphere in which you work. Below are a few suggestions to help foster an environment of respect.

1. You must have the mentality that everyone is important.

2. Treat employees in a consistent manner, and do not show favoritism.

3. Do not allow negative gossip to occur. If you hear, stop it immediately by saying something positive about the person being discussed.

4. You have to maintain a positive attitude and demand the same from your employees.

BELIEVE THEM AND BELIEVE IN THEM

How can you expect your employees to believe in you if you do not believe in them? The answer is simple, you can't. Believing your employees and believing in your employees must be standard operating procedures if you want to receive the same in return.

Believing your people basically means that you trust them until they give you a reason to doubt their honesty. You should give them your full trust from the minute that they are hired without requiring them to work for it. If you are hiring the right people, you should have no reason to doubt their intentions. Give this some thought the next time you are questioning one of your employee's motives. Are you giving them the benefit of the doubt?

What is the difference between believing your people and believing in your people? As we previously discussed, believing your people means giving them trust from the beginning. Believing in your people is much more than that. This means treating your employees as if they are advisors. You trust them enough that you want their input on critical decisions. You encourage them to have their own ideas and to share them with you. You defend them when their integrity

is in question by others. You must be their
number one supporter.

HAVE AN UNSELFISH ATTITUDE

Having an unselfish attitude can be
extremely difficult, because you have to
consciously avoid unintentional selfish acts.
This is a valuable way to show your appreciate
for your employees. In the world of business,
you can unintentionally take credit for something
that your team has accomplished, and this can
severely damage your relationships with your
employees. If your employees feel that you are
taking all of the credit for the success of the
operation, they may be less likely to assist you
with tasks in the future. Changing the way that
you state accomplishments can assist you in
showing that you care. Below I have listed an
example of how your wording can have a dramatic
impact on the message that is received.

1.   Example- Joe came up with an idea that helped save the business $5,000.

   a. Response 1- I just finished up the XYZ project, and the location will save $5,000. (Joe may interpret this as you taking the credit for his idea. Joe may never state his concern, but he may not bring his ideas to you in the future.)

   b. Response 2- I just finished up the XYZ project that Joe came up with and the location saved $5,000. Everyone take a minute to thank Joe for his great idea. (This response sends an entirely different message to the team, and this may not only improve your relationship with Joe, but other teams members may come to you with ideas of their own.)

Taking the additional time to show your employees that you care will pay off in the long run. As previously stated, you must have a genuine concern for your employees' wellbeing, show it on a consistent basis, treat everyone with respect, believe them, believe in them, and have an unselfish attitude. Practicing these techniques can improve your team's morale, improve attendance, decrease turnover, and improve results.

Your manager treats you with honesty and respect.

Honesty is Essential

You cannot put a price on the value of honesty. Without this characteristic, you are doomed to failure. Failure may not be immediate, but it will occur if you do not practice honesty on a routine basis. When I refer to honesty, I do not simply mean telling the truth. Being truly honest, means that you tell the truth, act with consistency, hold everyone accountable, and you do what is right instead of what is easy.

TELL THE TRUTH

Telling the truth in business can be difficult at times, because it is not easy to admit our mistakes and take the blame for our failures. The first step in changing this mentality is to realize that mistakes and failures are temporary bumps in the road to success. If you are not making mistakes and experiencing setbacks then I feel it would be safe to say that you are not attempting to make any progress. You have to fail in order to succeed. You must take ownership of your mistakes, and do not blame others or make excuses. By changing the way you view your setbacks, you will be more willing to admit them, learn from them, and move forward to success.

ACT WITH CONSISTENCY

Consistency was touched on earlier, but it cannot be discussed enough. It is important to treat your employees fairly, and you must avoid the impression of favoritism to maintain positive morale. You can help maintain consistency by having clearly defined requirements for each position and by holding every employee in that position to the same standard. If you allow one employee to slack off on a specific area then you are asking for trouble. Set the standards, require the standards from everyone, and consistently respond to each employee that is not meeting the standards.

HOLD EVERYONE ACCOUNTABLE

There are very few ways to lose the respect of your employees faster than not holding all of your employees accountable. If you do not hold all of your employees and yourself to the same high standard on a consistent basis, your employees may lose their belief in you as a leader.

You will quickly exhaust your top performing team members if you allow other team members to drop the ball and require the top team members to pick up the slack. It is great to have "go to" players, but if this is not handled with care, you may end up losing the employees that you value the most. The workload must be fairly distributed among the team members, and you must quickly address and resolve any issues with nonperformers to keep your top performing players from becoming overwhelmed.

DO WHAT IS RIGHT, NOT WHAT IS EASY

It is easy to say that you do what is right instead of what is easy, but it is human nature for us to take the path of least resistance. You must avoid this path at all costs, because you are responsible for setting the acceptable standards of behavior. When you are faced with a challenge, you must walk the walk or your team may lose trust in you. If you have consistently required them to handle a situation in a specific manner, you cannot shortcut the system when you are confronted with the same obstacle. You must handle the situation in the way that you require your employees to handle it to build their trust and respect for you. Keep this in mind the next time you are making a decision. Are you sending the right message?

You are encouraged to take calculated
risks to improve overall performance.

Eliminate Intimidation and Encourage Innovation

If intimidation is required in the
workplace, one of two problems exists. You have
the wrong manager or you have the wrong
employees. I believe that the first answer is
more often true than the latter. Have you ever
witnessed a business turn around a terrible
situation by changing nothing more than the
leader? What is the cause of this turnaround? I
am certain that there are numerous reasons why
this occurs, but none can be more important than
having a positive, innovate leader replace a
leader that leads by intimidation and fear.

ELIMINATE INTIMIDATION

Leaders that attempt to intimidate their
employees by threatening their jobs, micro-
managing, forcing them to do as they say without

question, and acting in a disrespectful manner will not maintain long term results. By placing a manager with this mentality into a struggling operation, you may see short-term benefits due to the increased structure, but these improvements will be short lived. As soon as the employees recognize this type of leader, they will go into a shell and perform the minimum requirements. Employees that are afraid of losing their jobs will only do enough to keep the manager off of their case. They will not be willing to come up with new ideas, because they fear the reaction they will receive when they present the idea or if the idea is implemented and is not successful.

ENCOURAGE INNOVATION

Encouraging innovation is an extremely effective way to "Permit" your team to achieve maximum results. Many times, the only thing standing in the way of unprecedented success is a manager that is not encouraging employees to

think for themselves. Who can better tell you
how a process works than the person who is
performing the process on a daily basis? That
person knows what is wrong with the current
procedures, and they probably already have ideas
to fix it. Your role is to encourage their
innovation.

Encouraging innovation does not mean taking
unnecessary risks. You still have the final say
in the direction that you take your team, but you
will have more paths to choose from. If you are
hiring employees that are smarter than you and
have strengths in areas that you are weak, why
would you force them to do as you say? You might
as well do everything yourself if you will not
allow your employees to come up with innovative
solutions on their own. By allowing your
employees to come up with ideas on their own,
implement those ideas, and give them credit for
their achievements; they will be more committed
to the cause, feel a sense of ownership, have a

greater respect for you, and they will be more willing to come up with solutions in the future. This is a recipe' for success!!

You receive adequate training and mentoring to develop you for future opportunities.

Don't Hold Them Back

The final step in building your employees' belief in you can be the most difficult. You have invested your time, energy, and effort to identify, hire, train, and develop your employees to take on more responsibility. When you have an employee that is ready and is offered an opportunity to take the next step; it is imperative that you do not hold them back from that opportunity. The first time that you stop an employee from advancing due to your lack of a contingency plan for business without them, you run the risk of seriously damaging your relationships with your top performers.

PREPARE FOR THEIR DEPARTURE

To soften the blow of losing a top-performing employee, you must prepare for their

departure before they are ready for a promotion.
You cannot allow your operation to rely so
heavily on one individual that you cannot
successfully operate without them. You must
identify each employee's replacement and develop
both employees simultaneously to prevent a gap in
performance. You should also maintain a list of
responsibilities for each employee in your
operation, how to perform those responsibilities,
and who has been cross-trained to complete those
functions. Planning ahead can give you the piece
of mind to know that you will not suddenly be in
a position that you cannot handle. This will
also give you the ability to simply congratulate
your employee on their promotion and release them
from their current duties. You would not be
where you are today if someone had not had belief
in you and given you the opportunity to advance;
therefore, you owe it to your team to do the same
for them.

Section 4: *Belief in the* *Cause*

Start with
their Goals

Agreement
Must
Occur

Cause

The
Vision
Must be
Clear

The Vision Must be
Attainable

Incremental Goals
Identified

Achieving the goals of the team assists me in achieving my own personal goals.

Start with their Goals

To develop belief in the cause, it is essential to start by identifying the individual goals and aspirations of your employees. If you are not taking your employee's best interests into account when developing your vision, it is destined to fail. It is possible to achieve short-term success by unconsciously developing goals that are in line with the goals of your employees, but to achieve long-term success; you must identify and understand each of your employee's goals and develop a plan to help them achieve their personal goals while executing the goals of the organization. This does not mean manipulating your employees to improve the organization for your benefit. If that is your intent, this will eventually be discovered, and you may lose everything that you have worked to achieve.

I am aware of the vision and fully understand it.

The Vision Must Be Clear

After determining the individual goals of each of your employees, it is time to develop a plan to help them achieve their personal goals and the organization's goals simultaneously. In order to be successful, it is important that every member of your team understands the goals of the organization. How can you help everyone understand the vision? Having a specific vision that is documented with identified variables, each team member's responsibilities assigned based on their strengths, incremental goals that are well defined, and an established time frame for completion can help increase each employee's understanding of the vision as well as increase their commitment to the success of the vision.

IDENTIFIED VARIABLES

What does it mean to have identified variables? Variables are the inputs that go into a process to create an output. By identifying each variable and assigning them with a weight based on the overall effect it has on the final output, you can identify and prioritize the areas requiring improvement much easier. This is a great tool to use when presenting the vision to your team, because you are providing your employee's with visual and verbal communication which can help increase their retention of the material. I have illustrated an example of identifying and prioritizing the variables below.

Variables (inputs) used to generate a Sell (Output)

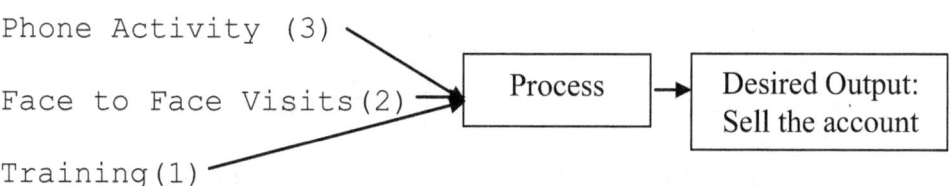

Phone Activity (3)

Face to Face Visits (2) → Process → Desired Output: Sell the account

Training (1)

As you can see from the illustration above, I have identified three major inputs that are involved in the process of selling an account. Assigning each input with a weight based on the influence that it has on the final output can help improve understanding and to drive your improvement efforts in the right direction. When you start working to improve a specific input (i.e. Training), you can follow the same process. This is illustrated below.

Variables (inputs) used to generate a trained employee (Output)

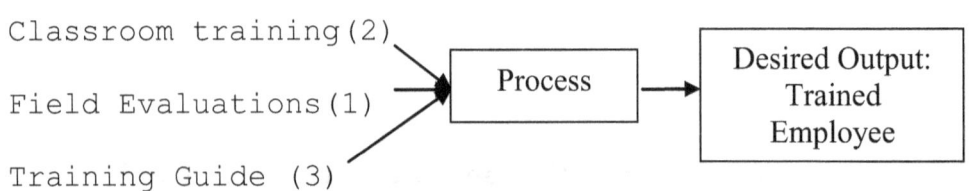

Classroom training(2)

Field Evaluations(1)

Training Guide (3)

Process

Desired Output: Trained Employee

As you can see from the illustrations above, you would focus on field evaluations to improve training which would in turn increase the likelihood of making the sell. This is very basic, but it helps you focus on the right areas.

ASSIGN RESPONSBILITIES BASED ON STRENGTHS

The second step to improving every employee's understanding of the vision is to assign responsibilities based on your employee's strengths (whenever possible). For example, if you have one employee that is great at typing and another employee that is great at presenting, it would not make sense to assign the typing duties to the speaker and the presentation duties to the typist. This may sound like common sense, but I have made this mistake in the past, because in the world of business, strengths and weaknesses may not be as obvious. Identifying your employee's strengths and weaknesses and assigning tasks based on their skills can greatly improve the efficiency of your team.

ESTABLISHED TIME-FRAME FOR COMPLETION

The final step to increase understanding of the vision is to identify and communicate the timeframe requirements for the primary goal and each incremental goal. If the team does not understand when the goal must be completed, they do not have a good chance of achieving it. This is one of the easiest steps to implement, but it is also one of the easiest to overlook. Take the time to establish the timeframes for completion and audit incremental goals along the way so you have the ability to change directions if required.

Top goals are broken down into smaller goals that are fully understood and a game plan is in place to improve each of these lower level goals.

Incremental Goals Identified

After you identify and prioritize your inputs and assign tasks to improve the inputs based on your employees' strengths, you are ready to develop incremental goals to keep the process improvement efforts moving in the right direction. Establishing incremental goals will give you the ability to track progress, reward/redirect employees, and give feedback along the way. This approach gives you the opportunity to proactively make adjustments to the plan as circumstances change and to keep your employees informed at all times. On the next page, I have listed an example of establishing incremental goals.

Primary Goal = Decrease Employee Turnover by 5% by January 1, 2011.

Incremental Goal 1 = *100% of Employees Fully Trained by September 7, 2010. (List Responsible Employee)*

Incremental Goal 2 = *Develop a Monthly Employee Goodwill Schedule by October 1, 2010. (List Responsible Employee)*

Incremental Goal 3 = *Set up an employee birthday card and anniversary card distribution schedule by September 15, 2010. (List Responsible Employee)*

As you successfully complete each of the incremental goals, you are moving one step closer to achieving the primary goal. The incremental goals can be viewed as check points on the road to achieving your primary goal.

The established goals are attainable.

The Vision Must Be Attainable

Developing an attainable vision does not mean that it has to be easy to complete. The vision can be extremely challenging, but it has to be possible in the minds of your employees'. As stated earlier, your employee's perception is their reality; therefore, if they do not belief that it is possible to accomplish the goal, they may be unwilling to fight through the obstacles and challenges that stand in their path to success. How can you develop a vision that your employees believe is attainable? The following areas should be reviewed when developing the vision.

1. Consistently Have Open and Honest Communication

    a. If your employees are afraid to give you honest feedback, you will be presented with many more challenges than a manager that practices open and honest communication. Your employees must feel comfortable telling you if you are making the wrong decision and/or taking the team down the wrong path.

2. Ask your employees what could prevent success.

    a. This is not planning for the worst to happen; it is planning to prevent the worst from happening, and if the worst does happen, knowing how to over-come it. Ignorance of the risks will not keep them from arising; therefore, it is better to identify them and plan to over-come them than it is to wait and be taken by surprise.

3. Employee's Scope of Responsibilities is Manageable

a. It is easy to make the mistake of
giving all of the important tasks to
a few key members of your team, but
this can hinder your chance for
success. If you overwhelm the top
performers, and you are not
challenging the remaining team
members, a once achievable goal can
seem impossible. Every member of the
team must contribute for the team to
be a success, and for each team
member to see the goal as achievable.

4. The Time-frame for Completion is possible.

a. If you have established a vision that
your team members agree is possible
to achieve; you run the risk of
leaving out one important element.
You must develop a realistic time-
frame for completion. You may have
the commitment from your team that
the goal can be accomplished, but you

must also gain agreement that it can be achieved in the time-frame that has been established. If you do not provide the team with enough time to achieve the vision; you run the risk of increasing frustration and decreasing commitment to achieving the goal.

The best idea wins instead of the leader dictating the direction.

Agreement Must Occur

At this point, you should already have a documented vision; including each employee's goals, incremental goals for the team, defined inputs, assigned responsibilities, and an expected time-frame for completion. You should have also determined the possible road blocks preventing successful completion of the goal and have a plan to over-come each potential obstacle if it arises. The final step to building belief in the vision is to gain agreement in a group setting from every employee. This will be easier to accomplish if you work to ensure that the best idea wins in debates with the team. We will review these areas below.

EMPLOYEE'S COMMIT IN GROUP SETTING

By establishing each employee's commitment in front of the other team members, it is more difficult for an individual to make negative comments about the plan of action since they were involved in it's development. Every team member will be an owner of the vision since they helped create it; therefore, they will be more willing to stick with it when times get tough.

THE BEST IDEA MUST WIN

The vision should not be about you or about any specific member of your team. Every team member is equally important, and you must select the plan that gives the team the best chance of success, regardless of who developed the plan. On a team, it is not about personal pride, it is about achieving the objectives. You have to welcome disagreements, have heated debates, and be willing to change directions, if necessary, in order for your team to be successful.

Section 5:
Belief in Self

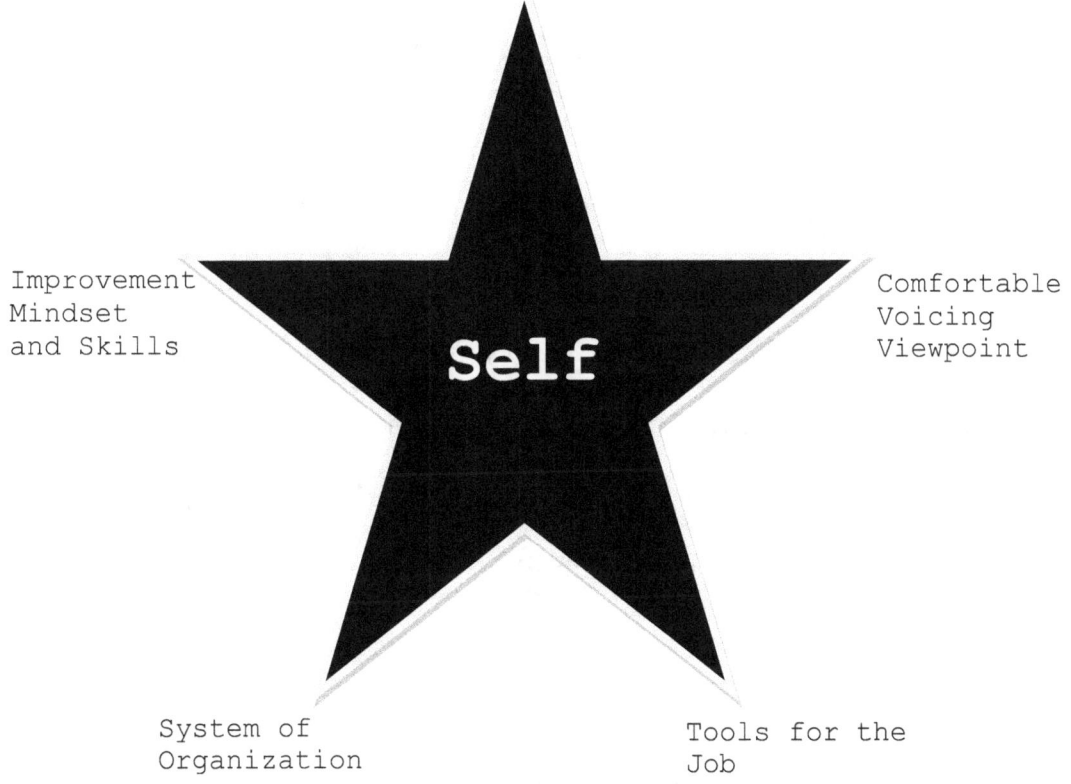

Adequate
Knowledge
and Skills

Improvement
Mindset
and Skills

Self

Comfortable
Voicing
Viewpoint

System of
Organization

Tools for the
Job

I have the knowledge and skill to successfully perform my job.

Adequate Knowledge and Skills

There are some employees that can achieve success without in-depth training and with little experience. They just seem to get it. It is great to find a person that is capable of making things happen on their own, but you cannot expect this from your employees. You owe them nothing less than your best effort, and you must work to ensure that they have the adequate knowledge and skills necessary to perform their jobs. By setting up an established training routine, scheduled mentoring sessions, and a documented evaluation system; you can increase your employees' knowledge and improve their job related skills.

ESTABLISHED TRAINING ROUTINE

What does it mean to have an established training routine? This basically means that training does not occur haphazardly. You must have a documented training guide to ensure that all topics of importance are being covered in the appropriate time-frame. It is not enough to simply create the training guide and assume that it is being followed. Having a documented control plan in place to ensure that the training remains on schedule is invaluable. For example, I have it in my personal routine to audit and evaluate the training compliance for each member of my team on a weekly basis. I can immediately identify areas that need more attention and help get training back on track if I am inspecting it on a routine basis.

SCHEDULED MENTORING SESSIONS

Scheduled mentoring sessions can be an excellent way to improve your relationships with your employees and to improve their skills at the same time. Your employees will appreciate the fact that you are a taking time out of your week to meet with them and to help them improve their performance. These sessions should be set up on a routine basis, and you must make sure that they consistently occur. Canceling these mentoring sessions could send the wrong message to your employees; therefore, it is imperative that you follow through with your commitments.

DOCUMENTED EVALUATION SYSTEM

After your employees complete the training program, it is essential that you have a documented evaluation system in place to determine their overall understanding of the material. By evaluating every employee on the same scale, you will get a better understanding of the areas of weakness in your training program, and you will be given the opportunity to spend more time with each employee on the areas in which they require more training.

CHANGE AS NEEDED

In business, changes occur on a daily basis; therefore, your training program must be evaluated and revised as circumstances warrant. One way to improve the quality of the training material is to give your recently trained employees the opportunity to give feedback and suggestions for improvement on the training procedures. Providing your employees with the opportunity to receive the appropriate knowledge and skills to confidently perform their jobs must be a non-negotiable part of your personal routine in order to achieve great success.

I am comfortable voicing my viewpoint to the team and to the leader.

Comfortable Voicing View-Point

As we discussed in section 3 (Belief in the Leader), intimidation may allow you to achieve short-term improvements, but it will prevent you from permitting maximum results. If your employees are not comfortable voicing their personal view-points, you are on the express lane to failure city. To increase the likelihood that your employees will give you their honest view-points, you have to start by changing yourself. You have to welcome constructive criticism and encourage your employees to tell you what could keep an initiative from being successful.

WELCOME CONSTRUCTIVE CRITICISM

You should have a strong enough relationship with your employees that you feel comfortable giving them constructive criticism, but this is only half of the equation. You must also be willing to listen to their criticism of you without allowing emotions to take over. As long as your employees are disagreeing with you in a respectful manner; you have to force yourself to listen and make changes if they are required. Welcoming constructive criticism can help you hold each other accountable, make changes when necessary, and improve your relationships with your employees.

REQUEST THEIR INPUT

The next area that can greatly improve your employees' willingness to voice their view-points is to request that they give it. In the past, I made the mistake of presenting a plan of action instead of discussing a possible plan of action.

There is a huge difference in these two approaches. The first approach assumes that I am right and that everyone should just follow my lead without question. I have not had much success with this approach. The second approach is much more effective, because every employee is involved and many mistakes can be avoided before they happen. Any time that I suggest a plan of action, I follow up by asking my employees what could stand in the way of successfully achieving the goal. If you try this approach, you will be amazed at the accuracy of their predictions. As the manager, you will have to make the ultimate decision, but it is foolish to move forward without consulting your team first.

I have the appropriate tools to perform my job, and I fully understand how to use these tools successfully.

Tools for the Job

Asking an employee to perform their job without the appropriate tools is like asking a baseball player to hit a homerun without a bat. It is the manager's responsibility to ensure that every employee has the right tools for the job and to train them to use the tools effectively. Before you can provide the right tools, you have to know what tools are required. You can help determine these requirements by asking top performing employees, communicating with new employees during their development, brainstorming with other managers, and by personally performing each job.

ASK TOP PERFORMERS

Top performing employees have figured it out. They know how to get the job done, and they do it right. They can be a valuable resource if you do not let your pride get in the way. Let them know that you appreciate their contributions, and ask them for help. Have each top performer put together a list of tools that they believe are required to successfully complete their job responsibilities. This will not only give you a great starting point, but it can help develop your relationship with your top performing employees.

COMMUNICATE WITH NEW EMPLOYEES

Do you communicate with your new employees during their development? If not, you are missing out on valuable information. These employees do not usually have bad habits to correct, because everything is new to them. By intently listening to their thoughts, questions, and concerns, you can identify areas that require improvements. For example, if several new employees have trouble understanding how to use a specific tool, you may want to increase the training time invested on that tool.

BRAINSTORM WITH OTHER MANAGERS

Another way to improve your understanding of the required tools for the job is to consult other managers in the same position as you. These managers should be presented with similar challenges, and they may have already developed tools to over-come those obstacles. By communicating with other managers, you can save a lot of time, energy, and effort, because you may not have to reinvent the wheel.

PERFORM THE TASK

Have you personally performed each job? There is not a better way to gain an understanding of the inner workings of each position than to perform it yourself. This does not mean that you have to spend weeks or months performing each job, but you must obtain a basic understanding by working on the front line with your employees. This can greatly improve your understanding of the requirements for each job while also improving your relationships with your employees.

I have a system to stay organized and ensure that I do not miss deadlines.

System of Organization

You cannot allow your employees to be unorganized. Unorganized employees will be stressed, inefficient, and they will negatively impact your team's overall performance. One big mistake that you can make as a manager is to assume that these employees simply do not care about getting the job done on time. They may have great intentions, but they may not know how to go about it. You should work to develop their organizational skills instead of working to remove them from the team. In the end, you may have to let them go, but this should not happen without giving them the opportunity to improve. If you lead by example, teach them organizational techniques, and provide feedback, you may be able to turn their good intentions into a reality.

LEAD BY EXAMPLE

You should not ask your employees to do something that you would not do yourself; therefore, it is imperative that you develop your own organizational skills and practice them on a regular basis. If your desk is cluttered, they may get the impression that this is acceptable; therefore, you have to work extremely hard to keep yourself organized first. By showing your employees that organization is a priority and proving that it can be successfully practiced on a routine basis, you have a better chance of getting your employees to follow your lead.

TEACH THEM HOW

The next step to improving your employees' organization is to teach them how to stay organized even with increased responsibility. To get to your current position as a manager, you have probably developed a method to keep yourself organized along the way. Spend time showing your employees how you personally maintain organization and provide them with training materials (books, seminars, etc) to improve their skills in this area.

FEEDBACK REQUIRED

The final step to keep their improvement efforts moving in the right direction is to provide feedback along the way. If your employees show improvement, it is essential that you praise them, because they will repeat behaviors that are rewarded. When their efforts fall short, it is just as important to help them get back on track. When you give feedback, it lets them to know where they stand, and it will keep them focused on making improvements. An organized employee will get more done in less time; therefore, it is worth your time to develop their organizational skills.

I have the confidence in myself to take educated risks to improve overall performance.

Improvement Mindset

Are your employees satisfied with their current results? Do they consistently develop ideas to improve performance or do they accept things the way that they are? These are important questions that must be answered. There are many reasons why employees accept current results instead of working towards improved performance, and the majority of these reasons can be over-come. Your employees may believe that change is difficult, they do not have adequate knowledge to make changes, they are not able to take risks, or they may not care whether improvements are made or not as long as they receive a paycheck.

CHANGE CAN BE DIFFICULT

Change is often difficult, but the cost of not making positive changes is much more painful. When businesses and employees refuse to change, they may be left behind or in circumstances that they are no longer capable of overcoming. As a manager, it is your responsibility to lead by example. If you are not willing to make changes, how can you expect your employees to change? An improvement mindset must be present from the top down; therefore, you should take a look at how you personally respond to change before moving forward.

LACK OF KNOWLEDGE AND SKILLS

As previously reviewed, it is imperative that your employees have adequate knowledge and the skills required to perform their jobs successfully. If your employees do not understand how to complete the basic functions of their jobs, they cannot make suggestions for improvement.   To develop an improvement mindset in each employee, you have to increase their understanding of their job first.   Invest the time to thoroughly train them, and give them the opportunity to improve the organization.

UNABLE TO TAKE RISKS

Are your employees allowed to take risks? If they are allowed to take risks, are they aware of it?   You may be able to answer this question yourself, but if you cannot, you can simply ask them.   For your organization to achieve and maintain success, you must encourage your employees to take educated risks on a consistent basis.   You can take this a step further by requesting their input on change initiatives.   If you encourage them to talk about their ideas for improvement and you respond constructively, you will make them more comfortable making suggestions in the future.   Start with the small stuff so they are prepared when something big occurs.

THEY JUST DON'T CARE

Do your employees care whether improvements are made or not? If the answer is no, many managers may start by replacing these employees, but I urge you to start by looking at yourself and the atmosphere of the organization. Do you practice an improvement mindset? Have you trained them properly? Have you encouraged them to take risks? If you cannot answer yes to each of these questions, the problem may not be your employees. This does not make you a bad person; it just means that you have some work to do. You may have to remove some of these employees from the organization, but you should first give them the opportunity to change. If the tables were turned, and you were the employee, wouldn't you want this chance?

Section 6: *Belief in the* *Team*

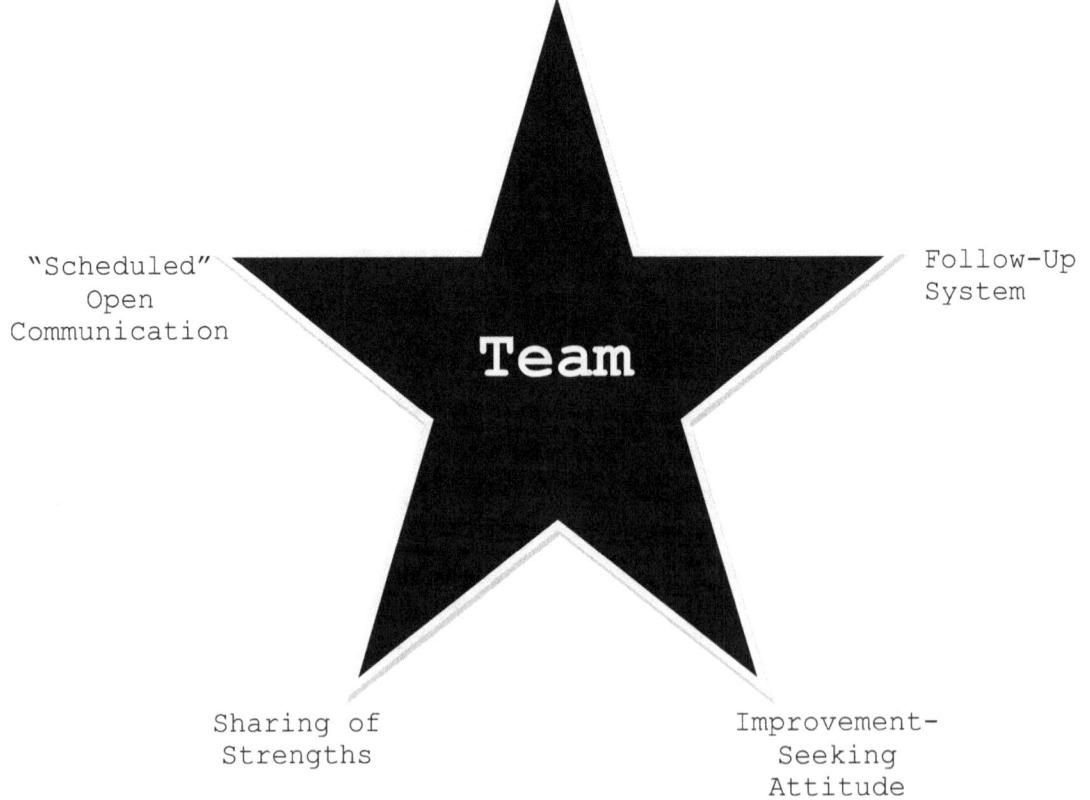

Right
Players,
Right
Positions?

"Scheduled"
Open
Communication

Follow-Up
System

Team

Sharing of
Strengths

Improvement-
Seeking
Attitude

Team members are in positions that are suitable for their knowledge and skills.

Right Players, Right Positions?

How successful would a football team be if the center and quarterback switched positions? Both of these players may be highly skilled, but they may completely fail when the requirements surrounding their positions are changed. Many managers believe that a poor performing employee should be removed from the team, but they may just need a change of position. Even if their new position is considered a demotion, making the change is in the best interest of the employee if it allows them to perform their responsibilities successfully. By changing their role, the employee may be more successful and move up the ladder faster in a direction that was not previously available. How can you determine what is the appropriate job for each employee? The following steps can help you put your employees in the most suitable positions: find out their professional goals, compare their strengths and weaknesses with the requirements of each position, and involve them in the process.

DETERMINE THEIR GOALS

Do you know what each employee wants to achieve on a professional basis? Determining where they want to be in the future can help you make sure that they are on the right path to get there. Employees are more excited about completing tasks that are moving them towards their goals; therefore, it is extremely important that you help them see the connection between their current job and how it relates to getting them to their desired position. If there is no connection, you may want to consider moving them to a different role.

STRENGTHS/WEAKNESSES SUITABLE FOR POSITION

Have you compared your employees' strengths and weaknesses with the requirements of each position? This is a useful step to help you determine if your employees are in the right jobs or if changes need to be made. As previously stated, if you have one employee that is great at typing and another employee that is great at presenting, it would not make sense to assign the typing duties to the speaker and the presentation duties to the typist. Make a list of the strengths and weaknesses of each employee and compare that list to the responsibilities for each job. This should make it much easier to decide what actions should be taken.

INVOLVE THEM IN THE PROCESS

Have you requested input from your employees? It is important to involve your employees in this process, because they can give you information about themselves that you cannot obtain without their assistance.   This will also increase communication between you and your employees, and it will help them realize that you have their best interests in mind.   If changes are required, they will be much easier to implement if you have involved your employees. This will keep your employees from being taken by surprise, and they will feel more comfortable discussing their concerns with you if the communication channels are already open.

Team members are dedicated to achieving the goals.

Follow-Up System Required

When employees feel that the other team members are not giving their best efforts, they may lose belief in the team. As a manager, you should allow your team to work with as little interference as possible, but you cannot give them a task and just walk away. A strong follow-up system must be established to ensure that everyone is contributing and that the project is moving forward at an acceptable rate. You can evaluate your current follow-up system by asking yourself the following questions.

1. Do you have scheduled one-on-one meetings with each team member?

    a. Scheduling one-on-one meetings with each team member will give you the opportunity to receive feedback from your employees. Employees may be willing to tell you things in private that they would not tell you in front of the team.

2. Do you have scheduled open communication with the team?

   a. By having scheduled meetings with the team, it will keep the team focused and moving in the right direction. These meetings should include an update on the current status of the project, and you should assign a minimum goal to be achieved by the next scheduled meeting.

3. Are the results of each team member and the results of the team visible to everyone?

   a. Displaying the results of the team as well as the results of each team member can have a great impact on participation. I believe that many employees on a team do not participate because they do not have to. If they can get the same rewards for a completed project without putting forth their best effort, they may do just that. By displaying the results of the team and each team member, every employee realizes that they can be held accountable for their contribution (or lack of contribution). You have to inspect what you expect.

Asking yourself the three questions above can help you evaluate your current follow-up system. You have to be careful to ensure that you are only following up and not doubling up. By following up, you are making sure that everything is moving forward as planned. If you are doubling up, it means that you are interfering to the point that work is being completed twice. You have to allow your employees to think on their own and complete their tasks independently. If you go back and redo all of the work of your employees, you might as well have completed the work yourself to begin with.

Team members are consistently working to improve the performance of the team.

Improvement-Seeking Attitude

It is essential to the long-term success of your organization that every employee is working to make things better today than they were the day before. An improvement-seeking attitude must be a requirement on your team. As reviewed in section 5: Belief in Self (Improvement Mindset), it is extremely important that every employee is working to improve their own results, but it does not stop there. Individual results are important, but the results of the team must come first. You can evaluate the improvement-seeking attitude of your team by asking yourself the following questions.

1. Do you personally have an improvement-seeking attitude?

   a. This attitude must start at the top. If you are satisfied with the current results, how can you expect any different from your employees. You must consistently communicate the vision and let your employees know where you want to go.

2. Do you recognize sacrifices?

    a. Are your employees encouraged to put the team goals before their own? If they make a sacrifice, do you make a big deal of it? Take the time to publicly and personally recognize employees that sacrifice their own goals to improve the team. This will be time well spent.

3. Do your employees know what's in it for them?

    a. Employees may see the benefits of successfully performing their own responsibilities, but what about the goals of the team. Have you helped them make the connection? Do they know how furthering the goals of the team can help them achieve their own goals? If the answer is no, invest the time to paint this vision.

4. Do your employees know the details?

    a. The difference between good and great is in the details. If your employees do not have a complete understanding of what you are trying to achieve, how can you expect them to make improvements? Find out their level of understanding and train accordingly. This will save you time in the end.

Team members are willing to share their strengths to improve the team's performance.

Sharing of Strengths

As a leader, your job is not to find perfect employees to join the team; it is to find employees that fit the team perfectly. You have to encourage the sharing of strengths to over-come individual weaknesses. This will allow the team to achieve results that may have been impossible for any team member to achieve on their own.

CHICAGO BULLS

A great example of this was the Chicago Bulls. It is true that they had the greatest player in the history of basketball, Michael Jordan, but he could not have done it alone. He was not surrounded by the most talented players in the sport, but they were some of the most talented players in the specific areas that were needed for the team to be a success. Each player made a contribution to the overall goal of the team. They sacrificed their own personal agendas and played together as a team to win six NBA Championships in eight years.

IDENTIFY STRENGHTS AND WEAKNESSES

Have you identified the strengths and weaknesses of each of your team members? Have you assigned responsibilities based on those strengths? By assigning employees to the roles that best match their strengths, you can give the team a much better chance to be successful. Take the time to review your current placement of team members to determine if changes need to be made.

Team members honestly and openly communicate on a regular basis.

"Scheduled" Open Communication

Have you placed the right players in the right positions? Do you have a follow-up system to make sure things are going as planned? Are you encouraging an improvement-seeking attitude? Are your team members sharing their strengths to over-come individual weaknesses? If the answer to each of these questions is yes, you have created an environment that "can" permit maximum results, but your work is not complete. The final step in the process of building belief in the team is having "Scheduled" open communication on a consistent basis. This communication process should consist of information exchanges, strategy sessions, and it must be on a routine basis.

INFORMATION EXCHANGES

Although information exchanges can, at times, seem trivial, they are vital to the success of any organization. As a manager, you may have information that you assume your employees are aware of, but what if they are not? How successful can your team be without all of the details? Even if these details seem like common sense to you, you still have to take the time to make sure that they are fully understood by everyone. Great success is in the details; therefore, your employees have to understand these details to have a fighting chance.

STRATEGY SESSIONS

What is a strategy session? This basically means to plan or to create a line of attack. When you are presented with a challenge, do you make a decision based on your strategy or your opinion? Creating a "plan of attack" will prepare you to make decisions that are based on fact instead of emotions when presented with challenges in the future. These strategy sessions should be held in two formats, both one-on-one meetings with each of your employees and with all employees in a group setting. These sessions should be documented with individual assignments that include a time-frame for completion.

OCCUR ON A ROUTINE BASIS

As we have discussed, it is important to have information exchanges and strategy sessions, but you cannot perform these events haphazardly. It is extremely important that these occur on a routine basis. Your employees will consistently be up-to-date on the details and the vision, they will be able to prepare questions and concerns, and they will feel more obligated to complete their assignments on time if they know when they will have to report the results.

Section 7: Belief of the Customer

The vendor provides a quality product/service that is needed by our company.

Product

What does the customer think about the products and/or services that you provide? Many times, we start by asking what we think about our products, but do our opinions really matter? Obviously it is important for us to believe in our products and services, but the most important factor is the belief of the customer. Without the customer's belief, we will not have a business to provide a product or service from. Ask your customers to evaluate the following areas if you want to know how your products/services stack up against the customer's expectations.

1. How would you rate the quality of the products/services that we provide to your company?

2. How effective are the products/services
   that we provide?

3. Do the products/services that we provide
   help your company accomplish your goals?

4. What changes need to be made to our
   products/services to improve your
   satisfaction?

The questions listed above are just a few of
the many questions that you may ask your
customers to help you determine how they view
your products and/or services. Develop questions
to gather feedback from your customers, because
their opinions are the most important to the
success of your business.

The vendor's products/services are provided at a fair cost to our company.

Value

After evaluating the customer's belief in your products and/or services, it is important to remember that a great product is not all that is required. What if you have the best products in the industry, but they are not affordable to the customers? The customer's perception of value is extremely significant to your overall success as a business, because if they are not able to pay for your product (regardless how good it is), your business will fail. The following two questions can help you evaluate your customer's perception of the value that they receive.

1. Are the products/services that we provide worth the cost that your company incurs to receive them?

2. Would your company prefer to sacrifice the quality and effectiveness of our products and services for cheaper alternatives?

These are a couple of the numerous questions that you could ask your customers to determine their perception of value. These questions may seem crazy to ask your customers, because you may fear that you will make them question the value that they are receiving. Just to clear up your concern, "THEY ARE ALREADY QUESTIONING THE VALUE WHETHER YOU KNOW IT OR NOT. DON'T YOU WANT TO BE INVOLVED IN THE PROCESS?"

For example, this question may not seem logical at first, but it is very important to ask. Would your company prefer to sacrifice the quality and effectiveness of our products and services for cheaper alternatives? You will find out the answer to this question in one of two ways. You will lose the business, because a competitor is able to provide them with a cheaper alternative. The other option is to proactively ask the customer. This will give you the opportunity to research and determine if you are able to offer a cheaper alternative since they are not as concerned about the quality and effectiveness of the products/services. The second option gives you the opportunity to keep the business and to improve your relationship with the customer simultaneously. It does not sound as crazy when you look at it from that perspective!

The vendor takes the time to make sure that we understand how to use their products/services effectively, and they proactively offer other products, services, and ideas to improve our company.

Simplification

After determining your customer's belief in your products/services and their perception of value, it is time to evaluate something that I call "Simplification". What if your product is the best quality product, the customer believes it is valuable to their business, but it is extremely complicated and they are unable to consistently use it effectively? In this scenario, you still run the risk of losing the customer to a vendor that can provide an easier to use solution. Use the following questions to evaluate the customer's belief in the "simplification" of your products/services.

1. Are the products/services easy to use?

2. Do you receive the appropriate level of support from our company to use the products/services effectively?

3. Do you require additional training from our company on the products/services that we provide?

By providing the customer with an opportunity to convey concerns that they have in this area, you are opening up the lines of communication, decreasing the likelihood that you will lose the business due to an easier to use solution from another vendor, and improving your customer's understanding of your products/services at the same time.

The vendor provides excellent service to our company.

Service

What is excellent service? How would you rate the service that you provide to your customers? How do your customers rate the level of service that they receive from your company? After reviewing the previous three questions, it is easy to see which one is the most important to the success of your business. It is important to have an understanding of what excellent service should be, and it is just as important to personally evaluate the level of service that you provide to your customers. Although the previous two points are extremely important, they will not pay the bills for your business. The customer's perception of the service that they receive is what really counts. Asking the customer the following questions can help you determine how the customer perceives the service that they are receiving.

1. How would you rate the level of service
   that you receive from your service
   representative?

2. How would you rate the level of service
   that you receive from our company's
   management team?

3. How would you rate the level of service
   that you receive when you contact the
   office with questions?

This is not an all-inclusive list of the
questions that you can ask your customers. These
questions are simply intended to give you an idea
of the types of questions that you should be
asking your customers. Find out how they rate
the service that you provide if you truly want to
improve your organization.

I trust that the vendor is honest and ethical in their business practices.

Trust

The most important step was saved for last so it will remain fresh on your mind. If you do not have the trust of your customers, your business will fail. This failure may not be immediate, but it will occur. It is essential that your customers believe that you and your employees are honest, helpful, enthusiastic, ethical, and that you value the relationships with your customers. You owe it to your customers to seek out their input on these areas, because you must have their trust in your company before you can achieve great results on a consistent basis.

Customers that trust their vendor are often willing to pay more for the products and services that they receive, they are less likely to give their business to a competitor, and they are more likely to purchase additional products and services from your company in the future.

Evaluate your customers' trust in your company by asking them some of the following questions.

1. Do you believe that our company is honest and ethical in our business practices?

2. Do you feel that our employees are helpful and enthusiastic when you come to them with a concern and/or question?

3. Do you believe that we value our business relationship with your company?

This list of questions could go on and on, and you will have to determine the appropriate questions to ask each of your customers. The point is simply that you must find out how they perceive your company. Do they trust you? Do they trust your employees? If the answers are yes, you are on your way to success. If the answers are no, make the appropriate changes, re-evaluate their perception, and get back on the road to success.

Section 8: Summary & Conclusion

SUMMARY

The purpose of this book was to introduce the "Theory of Belief" and to change the way businesses view their customers, their employees, and themselves. The power of belief in business is tremendous. Despite the effect that it has on the success or failure of businesses, it is often ignored or not even considered at all. By leveraging the power of belief, you can significantly improve your business' results and create a better work environment for yourself and your employees.

CONCLUSION

I have designed the following section of this book to help you implement these changes without having to review the book again in its entirety. This section is entitled, "Quick Reference Outline", and it contains the key points from each section throughout the book. I wish you all the best of luck today and in the future.

Section 9: Quick Reference Outline

I.   **Introduction**

   a. You can force your employees to perform the minimum requirements or you can allow them to achieve unprecedented success.

   b. People that are afraid to lose their jobs will only do enough to keep themselves out of trouble.

   c. Take the time to understand the power of belief and how it impacts the decisions of your employees and customers.

   d. Force yourself to look at every situation with the "Right" point of view.

e. Albert Einstein referred to insanity as doing things the same way multiple times and expecting different results.

II. A New Mindset

a. The Theory of Belief

    i. Belief has a large influence on the way that we respond to life's many challenging obstacles and on the decisions that we make each day.

    ii. As our levels of belief increase, we will sacrifice more to achieve the desired results.

    iii. As our levels of belief decrease, we will sacrifice less to achieve the desired results.

    iv. You can fight through setbacks, over-come obstacles, and succeed against the most difficult challenges if you continuously refill your "Belief Tank".

b. Taking the "Right" Point of View

    i. "IF YOU WANT PEOPLE TO ACHIEVE MAXIMUM RESULTS, YOU MUST STRIVE TO PROVIDE THEM WITH ALL OF THEIR NEEDS, BUT IF YOU WANT A PERSON TO PERFORM EVEN WHEN DEPRIVED OF THOSE NEEDS, THEY MUST HAVE A STRONG BELIEF IN THE CAUSE."

    ii. You must look upon any goal, obstacle, or challenge with the appropriate perspective.

    iii. Sometimes, your employee's obstacles and challenges may sound more like excuses than valid concerns and your customer's complaints may seem trivial, but their perception is their reality.

c. Five Points of Business Belief

    i. Belief in the Leader

    ii. Belief in the Cause

    iii. Belief in Self

        iv. Belief in the Team

         v. Belief of the Customer

III. Belief in the Leader

a. Get Staffed and Stay Staffed

         i. Create a documented vision of what you want to achieve. (Profit, Growth, etc)

       ii. Identify the type of person that you want to hire. (Personality type, Work Experience, Education, etc)

     iii. Rank your current employees and take the appropriate action steps. (Top, Middle, Bottom, etc)

       iv. Create a documented system to identify, recruit, and evaluate candidates. (Interview guides, job postings, testing, etc)

         v. Create a system to develop your employees. (Training, Mentoring, etc).

b. **Care about your People**

    i. Have and consistently show a genuine concern for your employees' well-being.

    ii. Treat your employees with respect.

    iii. Believe your employees and believe in them.

    iv. Have an unselfish attitude (i.e. Give credit where it is due).

c. **Honesty is Essential**

    i. Tell the truth.

    ii. Act with consistency.

    iii. Hold everyone accountable.

    iv. Do what is right instead of what is easy.

d. **Eliminate Intimidation and Encourage Innovation**

    i. Do not threaten jobs and micro-manage as a management style.

    ii. Do not force your employees to do as you say without question.

      iii. Give your employees the opportunity to think for themselves and to come up with innovate solutions.

      iv. Encourage your employees' creativity by requesting their input.

e. Don't Hold Them Back

      i. Prepare your employees to take on additional responsibilities in the future.

      ii. Prepare your business by creating a contingency plan for their departure.

      iii. Develop their replacement while you are developing them.

      iv. Congratulate your employee on their promotion and let them leave.

IV. Belief in the Cause

a. Start with their goals.

    i. Identify what is important to your employees.

   ii. Ask your employees what they want to achieve professionally.

 iii. Assign tasks and responsibilities that will prepare your employees for the future.

  iv. Explain how their current duties will help them achieve their future goals.

b. The Vision Must Be Clear

    i. Create a documented vision of where you want to go.

   ii. List the variables that affect the desired output.

 iii. Prioritize the variables based on the affect that they have on the desired output and select improvement efforts that start with the most important variables.

  iv. Establish a time-frame for

    completion.

c. Incremental Goals Identified

  i. Determine a primary goal with

    lower level incremental goals.

  ii. Use incremental goals to track

    progress, reward/redirect

    employees, and give feedback along

    the way.

  iii. Celebrate wins along the way to

    build momentum and to keep your

    employees focused.

d. The Vision Must Be Attainable

  i. The vision can be extremely

    challenging, but it has to be

    possible in the minds of your

    employees.

  ii. Your employee's perception is

    their reality. It does not matter

    if you agree with it.

iii. Consistently have open and honest communication to give your employees the opportunity to let you know if you are making the wrong decision and/or taking the team down the wrong path.

iv. Ask your employees what could prevent success. This is not planning for the worst to happen; it is planning to prevent the worst from happening, and if the worst does happen, knowing how to over-come it.

v. Ensure that your employee's scope of responsibilities is manageable.

vi. Make sure that it is possible to complete the task in the time-frame that you have allowed.

vii. The best idea must win. The vision should not be about you or about any specific member of your team. Every team member is equally important, and you must select the plan that gives the team the best chance of success, regardless who developed it.

e. Agreement Must Occur

    i. You should gain agreement from each team member on a one on one basis and in a group setting.

    ii. It will be more difficult for an individual to make negative comments about the plan of action if they were involved in it's development.

    iii. Make sure that every team member is an owner of the vision, because they will be more willing to stick with it when times get tough.

V.   Belief in Self

a. Adequate Knowledge and Skills

    i. Create a training routine and follow it.

   ii. Schedule mentoring sessions with your employees on a consistent basis.

  iii. Create a documented evaluation system to make sure that your employees understand the material.

   iv. Understand that change happens on a daily basis; therefore, your training program must be reevaluated and revised as circumstances warrant.

b. Comfortable Voicing Viewpoint

    i. Your employees need to be comfortable speaking their mind.

   ii. Welcome constructive criticism from your employees. You must be willing to listen to their criticism without allowing your emotions to take over.

    iii. Use their constructive criticism to make the required changes to yourself.

    iv. Request your employee's input on important topics. This will get them comfortable voicing their view-point since they know that you want to hear it.

c. Tools for the Job

    i. Before you can provide the right tools, you have to know what tools are required.

    ii. Ask top performing employees what tools they need to perform their job.

    iii. Communicate with new employees during their training.

    iv. Brainstorm with other managers that are in similar positions.

     v. Personally perform each task to better understand the requirements of the position.

d. System of Organization

     i. You cannot allow your employees to be unorganized.

    ii. Unorganized employees will be stressed, inefficient, and they will negatively impact your team's overall performance.

   iii. You should get yourself organized before you ask others to do it.

    iv. Teach your employees how to create and maintain a successful system of organization.

     v. Provide your employees with feedback along the way.

e. Improvement Mindset

     i. Change is often difficult, but the cost of not making positive changes is much more painful.

ii. As the manager, you must be willing to change or you cannot expect your employees to change.

iii. Train and mentor your employees to give them the knowledge and skills needed to implement positive changes.

iv. Make sure that your employees know that they are permitted to take risks. Let them know the boundaries.

v. Some employees may not care whether improvements are made or not. Start by looking at yourself first instead of immediately removing these employees from the organization. It may be the environment and not the employee, and you owe them the benefit of the doubt.

VI. **Belief in the Team**

a. **Right Players, Right Positions?**

    i. Determine the goals of your employees.

    ii. Put them in positions that fit with their strengths.

    iii. Involve your employee in the process, because they can give you information about themselves that you cannot obtain without their assistance.

b. **Follow-Up System Required**

    i. Schedule one-on-one meetings with each team member.

    ii. Have scheduled open communication with the team on a consistent basis.

    iii. Display the results of the team and the results of each team member where they are visible to everyone.

c. Improvement-Seeking Attitude

    i. You should start by making sure that you have an improvement-seeking attitude.

    ii. Take the time to recognize employees that sacrifice their own goals to improve the performance of the team.

    iii. Educate your employees on what is in it for them when it comes to team goals.

    iv. The difference between good and great is in the details. Find out each employee's level of understanding and train accordingly.

d. Sharing of Strengths

    i. As a leader, your job is not to find perfect employees to join the team; it is to find employees that fit the team perfectly.

ii. Encourage the sharing of strengths to over-come individual weaknesses.

iii. Identify the strengths and weaknesses of each of your team members and assigned responsibilities accordingly.

iv. Take the time to review your current placement of team members to determine if changes need to be made.

e. "Scheduled" Open Communication

i. This communication process should consist of information exchanges strategy sessions, and it must be on a routine basis.

ii. Information Exchanges

1. Even if the details seem like common sense to you, you still have to take the time

to make sure that they are
fully understood by everyone.

iii. Strategy Sessions

1. This basically means to plan
   or to create a line of
   attack.

2. When presented with a
   challenge, do you make a
   decision based on your
   strategy or your opinion?

3. These strategy sessions
   should be held in two
   formats, both one-on-one
   meetings with each of your
   employees and with all
   employees in a group setting.

4. These sessions should be
   documented with individual
   assignments that include a
   time-frame for completion.

iv. Occur on a routine basis

1. You cannot perform information exchanges and strategy sessions haphazardly.

2. By having these on a routine basis, your employees will consistently be up-to-date on the details and the vision, they will be able to prepare questions and concerns, and they will feel more obligated to complete their assignments on time.

VII. Belief of the Customer

a. Product

i. What does the customer think about the products and/or services that you provide.

ii. Questions to ask your customers.

1. How would you rate the quality of the

products/services that we

provide to your company?

2. How effective are the

products/services that we

provide?

3. Do the products/services that

we provide help your company

accomplish your goals?

4. What changes need to be made

to our products/services to

improve your satisfaction?

b. Value

    i. What if you have the best products

in the industry, but they are not

affordable to the customers?

  ii. The following two questions can

help you evaluate your customer's

perception of the value that they

receive.

1. Are the products/services

that we provide worth the

cost that your company incurs
to receive them?

2. Would your company prefer to
sacrifice the quality and
effectiveness of our products
and services for cheaper
alternatives?

3. You will find out the answer
by losing the customer or by
asking the customer.

c. Simplification

i. What if your product is the best
quality product, the customer
believes it is valuable to their
business, but it is extremely
complicated and they are unable to
consistently use it effectively?

ii. You run the risk of losing the
customer to a vendor that can
provide an easier to use solution.

iii. Use the following questions to evaluate the customer's belief in the "simplification" of your products/services.

1. Are the products/services easy to use?

2. Do you receive the appropriate level of support from our company to use the products/services effectively?

3. Do you require additional training from our company on the products/services that we provided?

d. Service

i. You must determine how your customers rate the level of service that your company provides.

ii. Asking the customer the following
questions can help you determine
how the customer perceives the
service that they are receiving.

1. How would you rate the level
of service that you receive
from your service
representative?

2. How would you rate the level
of service that you receive
from our company's management
team?

3. How would you rate the level
of service that you receive
when you contact the office
with questions?

e. Trust

i. If you do not have the trust of
your customers, your business will
fail.

ii. It is essential that your
customers believe that you and
your employees are honest,
helpful, enthusiastic, ethical,
and that you value the
relationships with your customers.

iii. You owe it to your customers to
seek out their input on these
areas, because you must have their
trust in your company before you
can achieve great results on a
consistent basis.

iv. Customers that trust their vendors
are often willing to pay more for
the products and services that
they receive, they are less likely
to give their business to a
competitor, and they are more
likely to purchase additional
products and services from your
company in the future.

    v. Evaluate your customers' trust in your company by asking them some of the following questions.

        1. Do you believe that our company is honest and ethical in our business practices?

        2. Do you feel that our employees are helpful and enthusiastic when you come to them with a concern and/or question?

        3. Do you believe that we value our business relationship with your company?

VIII. Summary

a. The purpose of this book was to introduce a new mindset explained by a theory of belief that should change the way businesses view their customers, their employees, and themselves.

www.ingramcontent.com/pod-product-compliance
Lightning Source LLC
Chambersburg PA
CBHW081126170526
45165CB00008B/2564